PICK YOUR BRAINS

about

SPAIN

Mandy Kirkby

Illustrations by
Caspar Williams & Craig Dixon

CADOGAN

Acknowledgements
The author and publisher would like to thank
'guest editor' Annie Young (aged 12).

A special thanks to Liz Bailey, for all her help.

Published by Cadogan Guides 2004
Copyright © Mandy Kirkby 2004

Illustrations by Caspar Williams and Craig Dixon
Illustrations and map copyright © Cadogan Guides 2004
Map by (TW)

Cadogan Guides
Network House, 1 Ariel Way, London W12 7SL
info@cadoganguides.co.uk
www.cadoganguides.com

The Globe Pequot Press
246 Goose Lane, PO Box 480, Guilford,
Connecticut 06437–0480

Design and typesetting by Mathew Lyons
Printed in Italy by Legoprint

A catalogue record for this book is available
from the British Library
ISBN 1-86011-157-2

John mcDonald

Contents

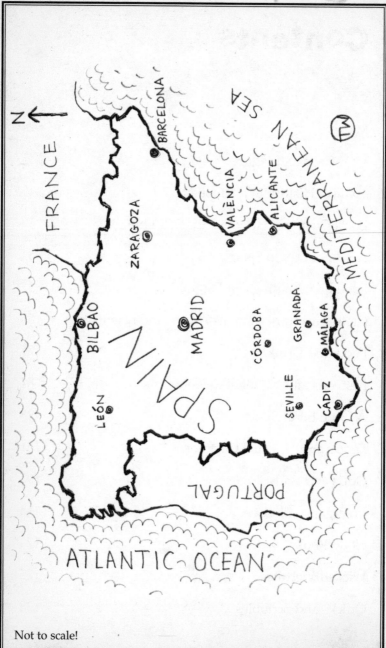

Not to scale!

Vital Facts
and Figures

Area: 505, 992 square kilometres (195,365 square miles). That's twice the size of Great Britain, with a little to spare.

Population: about 40 million. The population of Great Britain is about 60 million. They've got so much more space than we have!

Capital: Madrid. It has been the capital since 1561 and took its name from the Matriz, a little stream that ran through a valley. Hard to imagine now...

Major cities: Barcelona, Valencia, Seville, Zaragoza, Málaga

Oldest city: Cádiz, founded in 1100 BC. When England was at war with Spain in Elizabethan times, Francis Drake attacked Cádiz and 'singed the King of Spain's beard'.

Currency: the euro, which replaced the *peseta* on 1 January 2002. The *peseta* had been in circulation since 1868.

Internet domain: es

Time difference: Always one hour ahead of the UK.

Distances: London to Madrid = 1,670 km (1,038 miles)
Edinburgh to Madrid = 2,310 km (1,435 miles)
Dublin to Madrid = 2,220 km (1,379 miles)

¿¿¿¿¿¡¡¡¡¡¡Punctuation Alert!!!!!!?????

In Spanish, when you write a sentence that ends with an exclamation mark like '¡Feliz Navidad!' (which means Happy Christmas) you must put an upside-down one at the beginning. The same applies when writing a sentence with a question mark: an upside-down question mark must also go at the beginning of the sentence.

¡It may look a little unusual at first but you'll soon get used to it!

Borders: Spain shares a border with Portugal, France and Andorra. Morocco (in North Africa) is only 13km (8 miles) away across the Strait of Gibraltar.

Coastline: Spain has the longest coastline in Europe. It is surrounded by the waters of the North Atlantic, the Mediterranean and the Bay of Biscay. Did you know that you can see whales in the Bay of Biscay? A smallish whale known as the pilot whale. Lots of dolphins, too.

Regions: 17 independent regions. Galicia, Asturias, Cantabria, the Basque Country, Navarre, La Rioja, Catalonia, Aragon, Valencia, Murcia, Madrid, Castile and Leon, Castile-La Mancha, Extremadura, Andalusia, the

Balearics, and the Canary Islands.

Languages: There are four official languages. The main language, spoken everywhere, is Spanish. Catalan – spoken in Catalonia by more than eight million people; Galician –  spoken in Galicia (of course); and the Basque language, widely spoken in the Basque Country. You will see many street signs in Catalan and Basque (and a growing number in Galician). Catalan and Galician are similar to Spanish, but the Basque language bears little resemblance to it.

Geography: Central Spain (nearly half of the country) sits on a high plateau, which is crossed and surrounded by mountain ranges. Spain is a very mountainous country. In fact, it's the highest European country after Switzerland. The major mountain ranges are the Pyrenees, the Sierra Nevada, the Picos de Europa, the Sierra de Guadarrama and the Sierra de Gredos. The highest mountain in mainland Spain is the Mulhacén at 3,481 metres (11,426 feet) in the Sierra Nevada. Skiing is therefore a very popular winter sport and considerable amounts of snow cover the tops and slopes for several months of the year. The lowlands of Spain are around and between the mountains, areas such as Catalonia, Galicia, Valencia and parts of Andalusia.

The major rivers are the Ebro, Duero, Tajo, Guadiana and Guadalquivir; all except the Ebro flow into the Atlantic Ocean.

Climate: Spain is very hot during the summer months, especially in the south, where some of the highest temperatures in Europe have been recorded. The hottest day in Spain was 4 August 1881 in Seville when the temperature soared to 50°C (122°F). Summer in the south is also very dry and it might rain on only three days from June to September! Along the northern coast of Spain summers are not so hot and the weather can often be rainy and misty. Winters in the south are surprisingly mild and never reach freezing point, but remember that there are mountains and it does snow up there. In Madrid and central Spain, the summer can be scorching hot but it can get very cold during winter. On the Mediterranean coast, you'll find hot summers, mild winters and the warmest waters in all of Spain.

Travelling: Madrid, Barcelona, Valencia and Bilbao have underground systems. Look around for the sign saying 'Metro'. The railway network is called RENFE. Travelling by train is great fun, especially if you take the super-fast AVE train from Madrid to Seville. Buying a ticket can be complicated because there are so many different types to choose from. Go prepared!

Bus routes can be slow, especially in the countryside. Buy your ticket on the bus, but check with a local first – in small towns, a bar or café might be the place to buy one.

You'll see very few people on bicycles or mopeds. The Spanish LOVE their cars. They drive fast and sometimes break the rules, so be careful when crossing.

Spanish History in a Nutshell

Spain has been settled since 750,000 BC when the country was in the grip of an Ice Age, and prehistoric men and women first began to make their homes in the south, living in caves and hunting the woolly mammoth. When the Ice Age receded, primitive man began to look for new dwellings. Many different people and cultures evolved and, by the time the Romans invaded and conquered in 218 BC, Spain had long since been inhabited by a number of different tribes, including the Ibers – a short, dark race from whom many modern-day Spaniards inherit their black hair and dark complexion.

The Romans built new towns and cities, roads, aqueducts and bath houses, introduced the Latin language, from which the Spanish language evolved, and set about subduing and organizing the various tribes. The Romans called their new country *Hispania*, a name which eventually became España (Spain). *Hispania* is derived from the Latin word *Hispalia* meaning 'land of the rabbits'. When the Romans first set foot on their newly conquered territory, they were amazed by the large numbers of rabbits they saw, or so the legend goes.

After many centuries of rule, the Romans left Spain and a tribe called the Visigoths took over and began to establish a monarchy, as well as the beginnings of Christianity. But an invasion by the Arabs, hungry for Spain's riches, drove the Visigoths to the north of the country where they remained, preparing to fight back. The Arabs came from North Africa (a short hop by sea from the south coast of Spain) and are often referred to as the Moors because they came from a part of Africa called Mauretania (pronounced

'Moor-ee-tayneea'). By AD 718, they had conquered nearly all of Spain, renamed it al-Andalus and, like the Romans, brought new levels of learning and culture to the country. Everywhere you can see reminders of the Arab presence, especially in the architecture, in the use of ceramic tiles as decoration, in some cooking recipes, in words that were introduced into Spanish and in many of the place names. Apart from Sicily and southern Italy, only Spain amongst European countries has experienced such widespread Arab influence.

Slowly but surely, the Christians began to win back territory from the Moors, a long series of conflicts over hundreds of years, known as the Reconquest. It was completed in 1492. The Moors were largely driven

---

You can see the Age of Discovery and Golden Age Spain in:

☞ Seville cathedral, where Christopher Columbus is buried in a magnificent tomb.

☞ The palace and monastery El Escorial, just north of Madrid, built by King Philip II. He is buried in the royal mausoleum along with every Spanish monarch who has ruled since then.

---

away, although many stayed and converted to
Christianity. Spain was now a more peaceful country
although it consisted of several separate kingdoms. The
two most important were eventually joined together
through the marriage of Ferdinand of Aragon to Isabel
of Castile. The new Christian Spain ruled by a Catholic
monarchy eventually grew into the Spain that we can
recognize today.

Now a more peaceful and powerful country, Spain
meant business! It began to look beyond its own shores
and sent explorers to discover new lands. This was the
age of discovery and Christopher Columbus set sail in
1492 with three ships (the *Santa María*, the *Pinta* and
the *Niña*), a crew of Spaniards and one Englishman, all
of whom never expected to return. How wrong they
were! The discovery of
the New World (the
West Indies and
Central

—— *You can see Spain in trouble in:* ——

☞ the village of Miraflores de la Sierra, north of Madrid, where the annual fiesta begins with people walking around banging on saucepans and dishes. This is to commemorate the time when Miraflores was defending itself against Napoleon's soldiers and the villagers tried to make as much noise as possible to convince the enemy that there were more of them than there actually were!

America) and the subsequent conquest of Mexico, Peru, Chile, Ecuador and much of South America by the great conquistadors brought great wealth to Spain and turned it into one of the greatest empires of all time. The monarchy went from strength to strength and many influential marriages were made, including that of Catherine of Aragon to King Henry VIII of England in 1485 (she kept her head by the way).

The sixteenth century is known as Spain's Golden Age, the time when the country was at its most powerful. This period saw Madrid established as the capital city, and also saw conflict abroad, including war with Turkey, France and England and the famous defeat of the Spanish Armada.

Many of Spain's greatest painters and writers, including Cervantes, the author of *Don Quixote*, lived around this time and they depicted (and criticized) the grand and powerful times in which they lived. But by the end of the eighteenth century, Spain was in trouble. It had squandered a great deal of the fabulous wealth it had obtained from its colonies in South America, and a series of weak kings left the way open for the French Emperor Napoleon Bonaparte to invade in 1808. Fighting took place all over Spain as the people fought back. With the help of the Duke of Wellington's troops, the French were expelled in 1814.

The nineteenth and twentieth centuries saw more upheaval in Spain. The colonies in South America wanted their independence, fought for it and won. Back home, Spain was also in upheaval for most of the nineteenth century. Social and political unrest continued into the 1930s and the king called on the army for help. Eventually the military took control, the king was forced to abdicate and a republic was declared. The people of Spain now seemed in control, but there was conflict between the different political parties and war broke out – the Spanish Civil War.

It had a terrible effect on Spain: over half a million Spaniards died and many towns, cities and families were destroyed. Already a poor country, the war left Spain even more impoverished, so much so that ration cards were issued after the war. When fighting ended

---

You can see Civil War Spain in:

☞ the Reina Sofia art gallery of Madrid, where Pablo Picasso's famous painting *Guernica* is on display. This famous protest-painting depicts the catastrophic air attack on the town of Guernica, which was destroyed and where many civilians died. It is a powerful masterpiece.

in 1939, right-wing General Franco had won control and ruled the country until 1975 as a dictatorship, never holding a free election. When Franco finally died, Spain became a democracy and the monarchy was restored. Since then, Spain has gone from strength to strength and grown richer and richer, not just from tourism but from exporting all kinds of food and goods.

But you can put all that behind you and – like modern Spain – look to the future. In 1992, Barcelona held the Olympic Games and Seville hosted Expo '92, a world trade fair. This was an extraordinary year for Spain – the eyes of the world were upon it and it rose to the challenge.

Local Customs: How the Spanish Live

Spain is a large country, large enough for there to be enormous differences between the regions, but the one thing all Spaniards have in common is their sociability and the energy they put into enjoying life. They are a lively, noisy, expressive people who love children. Don't be surprised if you are patted and pinched and generally made a fuss over. Go with the flow!

In many places, people go out in the evening before dinner for what is called the *paseo*, a saunter around the town. The streets will be packed with people strolling along and chatting. You might see children acting out a bullfighting game using their hands as horns and their jumpers as bullfighters' capes, while people sit on benches playing a board game called *parchís*, a little like Ludo but played by everyone, not just children.

It would be a mistake to think that the sometimes chaotic and energetic way the Spanish lead their life means that you can break the rules and nobody will mind – that's far from being the case. The Spanish are very traditional, especially when it concerns the way people behave towards each other, and they place great value on having a close-knit family and doing the right thing. Family gatherings on a Sunday for lunch or an outing with grandparents, aunts and uncles are commonplace. Many

young people remain at home with their parents until they get married and students prefer to attend the university in their hometown rather than move away. This is not just because Spanish children love their parents so much, although that does play a part. It is more to do with the fact that, for many years, Spain was a poor country and young people simply couldn't afford to leave the family home. This way of life has continued despite the fact that Spain is now more prosperous.

When sons and daughters can finally afford to get married, the wedding will be one of the great occasions of family life and people will spend a great deal of money to ensure that the event is memorable. The bride will wear white, there will be bridesmaids and flowers, but the wedding ring will be worn on the right hand not the left, guests will give presents of money, as well as household gifts, and the groom will have his tie cut into little pieces!

Meet and Greet

The Spanish are very tactile, and shake hands and kiss much more than the Brits. People of all ages will kiss each other, once on each cheek, even if they don't know each other very well. If you are with a group of people, everyone must kiss each other hello and goodbye. It can take ages to get round to everybody! People don't kiss each other hello and goodbye at work though and, generally speaking, men give each other hugs and pats on the back on big occasions, like a wedding, or if they haven't seen each other for years and years. Men shake hands a lot, not just when they are being introduced to each other, but also as a greeting. Even young men and boys shake hands. It's very normal to do so.

The Spanish don't say 'please' and 'thank you' a great deal, but this doesn't mean they are unfriendly or that they don't think that being polite matters – because it does! When you meet someone, say *'Hola'* or *'Buenos días'*, it doesn't matter which. *'Buenos días'* means 'good morning' and, although it sounds quite formal to us, in Spain it is a very common greeting, not formal at all. If you see someone you know, and you can't stop to chat, then a casual '*¿Qué hay?*' will do. Translated, this means 'What's up?' When you say goodbye, '*Adiós*' is fine, although more and more people are saying '*¡Ciao!*' instead. It's up to you.

A Walk Down a Spanish Street

A Spanish street can be an assault on the senses – take a stroll down one and discover what different things there are to see.

Most people live in flats, often built around a courtyard, where you can hang out your washing and keep a few pot plants. Flats and houses tend to look very similar all over Spain, but in the countryside there are regional differences. A house in the north of Spain (where it can be very rainy) might have overhanging eaves so that water can spill down without collecting on the roof; in Castile you can sometimes spot timber-framed houses; and in southern Spain, there are houses of baked clay painted white to reflect the sun's rays. Very few people have gardens. It's difficult to grow flowers and keep the grass green when it's so hot, so instead, people like to grow geraniums on their balconies. If you hear some chirruping among the pot plants, it's probably the pet canary in its cage – they're very popular in Spain. In a quiet street, the whistling and singing of caged birds is a lovely sound. Spanish streets can look extremely pretty, especially if they are lined with orange trees. But they are not for eating as these are bitter oranges, grown only for decoration and to offer shade.

The outside of people's houses can often look dark and forbidding, with heavy doors and metal shutters on the windows as if there's no one at home. It's not you they want to keep out, but the sun. A great deal of Spanish life adapts itself to the rigours of the hot summers. Tiled floors (not carpets) are common in Spanish homes because they're so much cooler, and shady patios with little fountains can be seen everywhere. Shutters are often down throughout the day to keep the inside of the house cool. Many shops and offices close for a few hours in the afternoon when the sun is at its hottest and open again in the evening. Probably the hottest month of all in Spain is August, and many city- and town-dwelling Spaniards go to the

coast to cool down and have a holiday. They try to stay away for as much of August as they can manage, and many towns and cities can feel quite empty that month. A large percentage of Spaniards don't go abroad for their holidays and why bother? – the Spanish seaside is so warm and so beautiful.

The Spanish are very inventive craftspeople. Take the humble tile: you'll see them used for decoration on the outside and inside of buildings and to indicate street names. Huge tile pictures are very common in cafés and public buildings, very eye-catching, usually of scenes from the town's history, colourful images of

saints or even advertisements trying to sell you anything from cars to chocolate.

Religion plays a very important part in Spanish everyday life. There are churches everywhere, open daily and often well-attended.

The images of saints are displayed in cafés and shops; going to church is important and nearly every child is christened and confirmed. The great majority of national holidays and local celebrations have some sort of religious connection.

Spain in its Spare Time

There are many state-run and satellite channels to choose from and the Spanish are avid watchers of television. In addition, every region will have its own channel and make its own programmes. There's a great deal of sport to watch, especially football, also American films dubbed into Spanish, and many, many

soaps, often imported from South America. They're meant to be taken seriously but a lot of people think they're hilarious because they're so over the top.

There are several celebrity gossip shows with TV presenters sitting around talking about who's going out with whom. The Spanish are great lovers of gossip. Not surprisingly, *Hello!* magazine first began in Spain where it is called *¡Hola!*

You won't find as many dramas and serials as there are on British television and Saturday night is dominated by an all-singing, all-dancing spectacular, with comedy sketches and top performers – it goes on for hours!

Children's programmes are broadcast only in the mornings at breakfast time, sometimes on Saturday mornings and at lunchtimes (some schools have very long lunch hours). You'll recognize some of the programmes because many of them are shown on British television, too – lots of American and Japanese cartoons, Disney, even *The Tweenies* – all with Spanish voiceovers. A very recent popular Spanish cartoon from Barcelona was called *Las Tres Mellizas* – 'The Triplets' – and was the story of triplets who somehow found themselves in fairy stories, in Little Red Riding Hood or Cinderella, for example, and managed to change the endings of the stories! It's great fun.

The programme which recently broke all records was Spain's version of *Pop Idol* called '*Operación Triunfo*'. Practically the whole country watched it, not just young people, and this is probably because everybody in Spain listens to pop music and even parents were interested to find out who the next great popstar was going to be.

Even though we have *Pop Idol* in common, the music scene in Spain is quite different from ours. Whereas we tend to listen to British and American music only and don't really pay much attention to bands who sing in languages other than English, the Spanish are more adventurous than us. Their own homegrown music is probably their favourite but British and American bands are extremely popular – and they're singing in a different language! When you're in Spain, look out for David Bisbal (like Gareth Gates, he was the *Pop Idol* runner-up), Enrique Iglesias and a group called *La Oreja de Van Gogh* (translated that means 'Van Gogh's Ear'!). They're all huge stars.

Bands and singers from Latin America are a huge influence on the Spanish pop scene. Latin America is the collective name for the countries in South and Central America (Colombia, Argentina, Mexico, for example) that made up Spain's empire. Although these countries have been independent of Spain for some years now, there is still a strong link between them. They speak the same language – Spanish. The Latin American influence is very widespread in Spain and it is not just confined to music. You'll come across many Latin

Americans living and working in Spain, you might see books by bestselling Latin American writers like Isabel Allende and Gabriel García Márquez and you might be in a café and a very funny and slightly silly Latin American soap might be on the television.

When most people think of Spanish music and dance, they think of flamenco, which is a very dramatic dance with lots of foot-stomping and graceful arm movements, accompanied by singers, guitarists and drummers (the word *flamenco* refers both to the dance and to the music). Dancers wear a traditional Spanish costume – the women in long, flowing dresses (often with huge polka dots on them) and the men in tight trousers and short jackets. It is as typically Spanish as bullfighting and originated in southern Spain among the gypsies. The songs are usually about love gone wrong and life being hard! Nowadays, great flamenco dancers and singers are idolized all over the world and earn a great deal of money.

Not everybody in Spain listens to flamenco or can perform the dance correctly but everyone listens to music called flamenco fusion and can dance the *sevillana*. Flamenco fusion is a more poppy, jazzy kind of flamenco music that is extremely popular, often making it to the top of the charts. You might come across the Flores Family, a famous singing group (they're all related) in which every single member performs a different kind of flamenco fusion. The *sevillana* is a dance very similar to flamenco but which is easier to perform. Absolutely everybody in Spain can do the *sevillana* because they are taught how to do it at school from a very young age. You'll see people (men and women, boys and girls) dancing the *sevillana* at weddings and *fiestas* and almost anywhere where people gather to have fun. Little girls will often be wearing their lovely long, spotty flamenco dresses.

A School Day in Spain

Going to school in Spain isn't so very different from going to school in the UK. The day lasts from nine until four, sometimes longer, exams are taken at the ages of 16 and 18 and you can leave school at 16 if you wish. There is no school on Saturday and there are lots of after-school clubs to go to if your parents work. The same subjects are taught, although English is compulsory right from primary school. There are some differences though:

You start school the year you turn three. If the school term begins before you are three, then you must still attend, aged two! It is a little like nursery school so it's not too much of a shock although the hours are still school hours.

Little children are taught numbers and the letters of the alphabet in a very special way – before they learn how to write them down on paper, they must first make the shape of the number or letter with their bodies. For instance, the letter 'T' is made by standing with your arms stretched out either side of you. This method is called the morphological method (in Spanish, *método morfológico*) and it works!

What's so great about Barcelona?

Fountain in Parc de la Ciutadella

Fundació Joan Miró

Is it all the amazing things to see and do?
Is it the beaches?

Aquarium

La Barceloneta

35

Fabulous
Buildings
and Sights

The Sagrada Familia in Barcelona

Barcelona has some of the most bizarre buildings in the world, many of them designed by an architect called Antonio Gaudí. His most famous building is a huge church called the Sagrada Familia (The Holy Family). It was unfinished in the 1920s when Gaudí died and is the most unconventional church you're ever likely to see, with colossal, weirdly shaped towers decorated with coloured mosaics, and the walls, inside and out, are covered in hundreds of strange carvings of plants and animals. The reason why Gaudí's buildings are so strange is because he wanted to break with the convention that walls must be straight, churches must look like churches, and office blocks like office blocks. He certainly broke all the rules in a most spectacular way!

The Guggenheim Museum in Bilbao

This building, known to the locals as 'the Guggen', is ultra-modern, incredibly daring and dominates the traditional buildings that surround it. Built in 1987, the Guggenheim is a gallery of modern art, but many people spend more time

staring at the amazing exterior –
it's shiny, made of titanium and
sculpted into, well…it could be
a ship or it could be a fish or
any number of things,
depending on how your
imagination
works. At the main
entrance, don't
forget to look out
for *Puppy*, a huge
model of a dog
with a coat of real,
growing flowers.

La Giralda in Seville

The bell tower of
the cathedral in
Seville, known as
La Giralda, was
built in the twelfth
century by Moorish kings. It is incredibly high and yet
easy to climb because the stairs are very wide and
shallow. The steps were built this way so that the king
could ride his horse all the way up the tower to look at
the view and watch out for enemies. Look out for an
enormous revolving weathervane on the top. The tower
gets its name from the word *giraldilla* which in Spanish
means 'weathervane'.

The Alhambra in Granada

The Alhambra is a Moorish palace and fortress perched high on a hill just outside the city of Granada. Granada saw the end of Arab rule in Spain when the last king handed the keys of the city to the Christian monarch in 1492. Legend has it that the Arab king burst into tears and was told off by his mother! The name 'Alhambra' means 'red castle'. Its walls are built of a reddish clay extracted from the hill on which it stands. There are

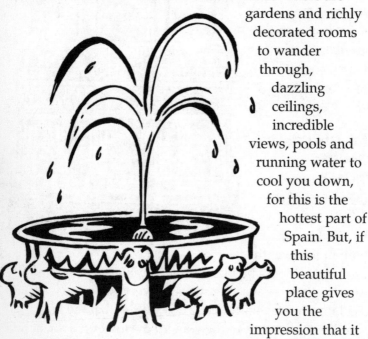

gardens and richly decorated rooms to wander through, dazzling ceilings, incredible views, pools and running water to cool you down, for this is the hottest part of Spain. But, if this beautiful place gives you the impression that it has only seen calm and untroubled times, then you are very mistaken. It has an incredibly gruesome past and centuries ago in one part of the palace, a rival noble family was massacred as they tucked into a lavish banquet. Look out for the tower, which was used as a signal post for sending messages, the palace baths and the lovely goldfish pond in the Court of the Myrtles, where the Moors would sit and eat ices made with snow from the tops of the Sierra Nevada mountains. Oh yes, and don't forget the harem!

TOROS BRAVOS

Spain's Jurassic Park

In the region of La Rioja, you can see enormous dinosaur footprints embedded in rock exactly as they were made 120 million years ago when Spain looked very different from how it looks today. It was wet and marshy! Look for signs near the villages of Encisco, Préjon and Valdecevillo.

Ronda's Bullring

Built in 1785, this is one of Spain's oldest bullrings, and it is the ambition of every young matador to fight here one day. No matter what you feel about the rights and wrongs of bullfighting, you will find it a fascinating and atmospheric place – the passion of the crowd, the bravery of the matadors and the drama of the fight are easy to imagine. In September every year, people flock to Ronda from all over Spain to see spectacular bullfights with the matadors in eighteenth-century dress. Millions of others watch it all on television. Don't miss the bullfighting museum with its displays of brilliantly coloured matador costumes!

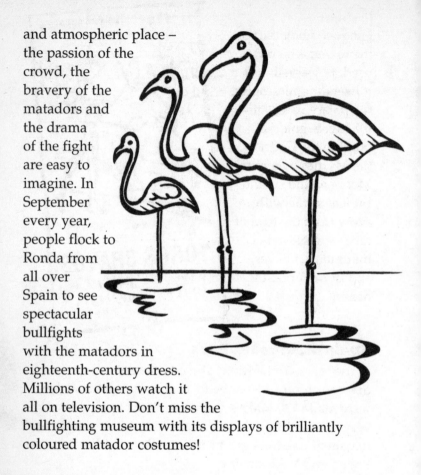

To the Top of Tibidabo

Just west of Barcelona lies Tibidabo, a peak 550 metres (1,804 feet) high. A little railway (called a funicular) carries you up the side of the slope to the top, where there are incredible views across the sea to Mallorca, over to the Pyrenees and down onto Barcelona itself.

Also on Tibidabo, there's an amusement park with some breathtaking rides.

Doñana National Park

Once a duke's hunting ground, Doñana is Spain's largest national park at the mouth of the River Guadalquivir, a huge area of lagoon, marsh, forest and some spectacularly high sand dunes. Thousands of birds live here – storks, spoonbills and pink flamingo – and roaming through the forest are wild boar, red deer and the extremely rare and rather shy lynx cat. Look upwards for the imperial eagle, soaring high up in the sky, its beady eye trying to catch sight of a rabbit for its next meal. The wildlife here is very special so it mustn't be disturbed and therefore you are only able to see some of it in the company of a guide. An alternative is to take a day-long boat trip down the river from Seville.

The Walled City of Avila

The medieval walls around Avila are unique in Europe: one mile long, totally complete, with 88 towers (on which storks can often be seen nesting) and nine gates. They were built in the eleventh century as defence against the Moors and made the city virtually impossible to attack. Avila is on Spain's high central plateau (in the winter, it can be cut off by snow) and many towns and cities in this part of the country have fortresses and high walls. They were part of the fortifications built to fight the invading Moors.

The Escorial

The Escorial is a magnificent royal palace and
monastery, just north of Madrid. It was built in the
middle of the sixteenth century by King Philip II,
perhaps the most well-known of Spanish rulers. He
was extremely clever, very religious, ruthless and
warlike – in fact, a genius! He sent the Spanish Armada
(the royal naval fleet) to invade England, he showed no
mercy to the people of South America, whose riches
the Spanish had plundered, and was ruthless towards
many of his fellow Spaniards who did not share his
Catholic beliefs.

The Escorial is an extraordinary place – it's huge and
imposing with 2,675 windows, 1,200 doors, 86
staircases, a library of 40,000 books and a sumptuously
decorated church. It was built to the king's exact
specifications: Philip consulted astrologers as to the
date when the first stone should be laid down, insisted
that the architect's designs be based on strange,
magical numbering patterns, and was so religious that
he had his bedroom built right above the church altar
with a spyhole to watch all the services going on down
below. Philip died here and is buried in a marble
mausoleum. The monarchs who succeeded him are
buried alongside in elaborate funerary urns.

The Roman Holiday Resort of Mérida

Mérida has more Roman ruins than anywhere else in
Spain and it was here that the conquering Romans went
to have fun. There are so many buildings here associated

with entertainment: a magnificent theatre complete with a stage set built from stone and granite, an amphitheatre where gladiator fights took place, and where you can still see the water channels that would have flooded the arena for staging mock naval battles. As well as the remains of a racecourse, there are the traces of many taverns and guesthouses where visitors would have found something to eat and a place to sleep.

The Strange Lunar Landscape at Tabernas

Tabernas is a town situated in one of the near-desert areas of Spain. The landscape here is very strange indeed – rugged, desolate, with dried-out riverbeds and cacti everywhere. It looks so much like the American Wild West that many famous spaghetti westerns were filmed here in the 1960s and 1970s. The stage sets were left behind and you can watch (and join in) the re-enactments of bank hold-ups and see stuntmen in cowboy fights. The desert landscape is

still used
for television
commercials and
even by film directors as
famous as Steven Spielberg.

Castles in Castile

When the Moors invaded Spain, the Spanish Christians
managed to keep hold of an area north of the region of
Asturias and frantically built castles to keep the
invaders at bay. When the Christians began to fight
back and drive the Moors southwards, they built even
more castles, so many in fact that the region was
named Castile (the Spanish for 'castle' is *castillo*). They
were usually built on hilltops so that people could see
for miles across the plains and, as a result, looked
dramatic and forbidding against the skyline. There are
2,000 castles in Spain, many of them in Castile so you
are spoilt for choice. Here's a selection:

☞ **Peñafiel**, on the crest of a hill overlooking the River
Duero, is an example of the type of castle known as the

'Great Ship' because of its shape. It looks like a huge battleship!

☞ **La Mota**, near Valladolid, was originally a Moorish castle. On some areas of the wall, there are stone overhangs, where boiling oil and other missiles would be balanced before being tipped over the enemy.

☞ **Coca**, near Segovia, was the stronghold of a local family, the Fonsecas. Its bricks are rose-tinted and look so decorative that it seems as if it was never intended to see battle.

☞ **Belmonte,** near Cuenca, was built in the fifteenth century and has massive rounded turrets. It is one of the best preserved in the region.

La Font Màgica

If you're in Barcelona, you mustn't miss the summer evening spectacular light-and-music displays of the Magic Fountain. Quite possibly the most amazing fountain you'll ever see…

Santiago de Compostela

In the Middle Ages, the cathedral of Santiago de Compostela was the most visited place in Europe. This was because one of Christ's Apostles, St James, was buried there. For many years, his tomb had been forgotten until in 813, a shepherd rediscovered it and spread the word. At that time, Spain was ruled by the

Moors but the Spanish were beginning to fight back, and it was said that the vision of St James kept appearing on battlefields to give the Christians encouragement.

St James became a very important figure and a great cathedral was built in his honour. He eventually became the patron saint of the whole of Spain. Pilgrims flocked to Santiago from all over the country and as far afield as France, often walking hundreds of miles across the mountains. Over the years, a special pilgrim road was established called the *Camino de Santiago* (the Way to Santiago). In fact, the world's first travel guide was written for the pilgrims of Santiago, giving advice on where to stay and where not to drink the water. Churches and cathedrals sprang up alongside the road where weary pilgrims could rest and pray. Hospitals were built (many went to Santiago to be cured of illnesses or were taken ill on the way) and even a bridge was erected by royal decree so that they didn't have to wade across a river. The pilgrims would often carry a long staff, wear a cape and a felt hat adorned with scallop shells, the symbol of St James. The scallop can be seen everywhere in Santiago and the areas

surrounding it. There's even a small church along the coast in a town called Atocha which has a roof covered in real scallop shells.

On reaching the majestic, towering cathedral, pilgrims would walk through a magnificent carved door called the Doorway of Glory (*La Puerta de la Gloria*), where they would find the statue said to impart wisdom if touched with one's forehead. The faithful would then pray and give thanks for a safe journey. The pilgrim road is still used today by those who walk it for religious reasons like the pilgrims of yesteryear and by those who want to see the beauty of the scenery along the way. If you travel all the way from France, it's over 750km (466 miles) long.

Everywhere you go in Santiago de Compostela there are reminders of its importance as a place of pilgrimage – the magnificent cathedral, the main square (one of the biggest you'll ever see) which was a meeting place for the pilgrims, the monasteries and the old hospital which would have given them help and somewhere to stay. Everywhere you look you'll see the scallop shell. If you're there on St James's Day (25 July), you can celebrate with the delicious St James's Tart (*la tarta de*

Santiago), an almond tart dusted with icing and a little image of St James's two-handled sword on the top.

Places to Take a Stroll

El Rastro Market

Every Sunday, hundreds of people visit Madrid's famous flea market, the Rastro. It runs the whole length of a very long street and spills out into the side roads as well. It has hundreds of stalls and it is said that you can buy almost everything here from second-hand clothes to a new dog. It's great fun to watch people bargaining and arguing, and to spot some of the crazier things people are trying to sell.

Time to spare?

☞ If you've got some time to spare after visiting the Rastro, there are two other Sunday markets in Madrid: a coin and stamp market in the main square, the Plaza Mayor; and close to the main park, the Parque del Retiro, there's a market selling books and magazines, some for children. There's often a little stall selling freshly-cooked crisps too.

Las Ramblas

This is the most famous avenue in Barcelona, lined with fabulous shops and things to see and do. Grand houses, a waxworks museum, a theatre, flower stalls, cake shops, a bird market, a colourful mosaic pavement, out-of the-way squares, Art Nouveau buildings, buskers and 'human statues'. There are other avenues branching off the main street and they are busy all day, every day. Sit outside a café and watch everyone go by. Don't forget to look out for the colourful dragon with his brolly projecting out from an old building which used to be an umbrella shop.

The World's Loveliest Henhouse

On the pilgrim road to Santiago de Compostela, there is a cathedral which contains the most beautiful henhouse in the world and has an extraordinary story to go with it. St Domingo lived in the town of Santo Domingo de la Calzada – named after him. A holy place, pilgrims would often stop here to worship at the cathedral. Centuries ago, a man and his parents were travelling to Santiago and stopped to rest. A young woman took a fancy to the son and wanted to marry him, but he refused and out of spite she accused him of being a thief. He was promptly arrested and hanged. His unhappy parents carried on to Santiago but on their return journey, saw that their son was alive and well, brought back to life by the miraculous powers of St Domingo. They rushed to tell the judge who had condemned him but he didn't believe them. He then looked down at his plate of two roast chickens and declared that they were as alive as their dead son. Suddenly, the chickens came alive and flew away! Ever since then, a live cock and hen have lived inside the cathedral in their lovely henhouse, decorated with beautiful ironwork and elaborate paintings of chickens.

The Hanging Houses of Cuenca

Cuenca is an old fortified city in Castile, built on a huge, high rock and it is famous for its ancient 'hanging houses', built on the edge of the steep cliff face. A few of them have been restored and you can go inside and stand on the balconies and look at the massive drop down below. What a place to live – better not be scared of heights!

New and Old Windmills

There's a lot of wind in Spain! If you travel through Zaragoza, you can't fail to notice row upon row of wind turbines on top of hills and stretching out across the plains. They are very striking and can be seen for

miles around.
Spain
generates a
great deal of
its
electricity
in this way.

In the old
days,
windmills
looked very
different and
were not used
for
generating electricity, that's for sure. The town of
Consuegra in La Mancha is famous for its 11 white
windmills all in a row on top of a ridge. When it's
harvest time, the only working windmill is set in
motion to celebrate a successful year's crop of saffron.
This is the world's most expensive spice, made from
the red stamens of the purple crocus. It is added to
paella to give it its yellowy-orange colour. All around
Consuegra, the fields are lilac-coloured when the
crocus is in flower.

Fauna in Madrid

The Spanish call this a 'biopark'. Ever come across that
term before? Probably not, because this is a unique
place. Over a vast area, it recreates the different
environments of the world – the polar region, the

tropical rainforest, desert, Mediterranean woodlands, the forest at night and lots more. With over 4,000 animals and 15,000 plants, Faunia manages to be true to life, and you'll notice this straight away when you enter the polar region – it's freezing! You can also visit a hospital for sick animals.

The Hercules Lighthouse

This enormous stone lighthouse on the coast at La Coruña is the oldest continuous working Roman lighthouse. A great deal of the stonework was rebuilt in 1791 but at its heart, it's Roman through and through. The coastline around here is known as 'The Coast of Death', a reminder of its many shipwrecks and drownings. Climb up the 242 steps of the lighthouse and look out across the ocean. See any shipwrecks?

Great Inventors, Famous Artists and Scientists

Some Spanish firsts
Chocolate
It is said that the great conquistador Hernán Cortés tasted a chocolate drink at the court of the Aztec king, Montezuma, in the sixteenth century and thought that his fellow Spaniards should try it too. Cocoa beans were shipped back to Spain and chocolate became a drink for the wealthy and fashionable, eventually spreading in popularity throughout

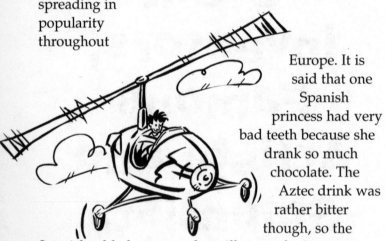

Europe. It is said that one Spanish princess had very bad teeth because she drank so much chocolate. The Aztec drink was rather bitter though, so the Spanish added sugar and vanilla to make it sweeter. Later, they developed the idea further and made solid chocolate.

The Autogyro
An early version of the helicopter, the autogyro was designed by the aeronautical engineer Juan de la Cierva in 1923. It was essentially a small plane with propeller blades on the top and, unlike today's

helicopters, it had to race along a runway before it could take off. De la Cierva came to Britain to show the autogyro to the Air Ministry to see if they would be interested in helping him develop the idea further. They were very keen and agreed to help. The little helicopter was used for military purposes and, believe it or not, to take a camera into the air and film the 1936 Cup Final at Wembley! Sadly, its inventor died in 1936 when he took one out for a flight and it crashed.

The First Submarine

The first submarine in the world was built in 1859 by an inventor called Narcisco Monturiol. He called it the *Ictineo*, which roughly means 'new fish'. Jules Verne based his fictional submarine, the *Nautilus*, on this new invention when he wrote his famous book, *Twenty Thousand Leagues Under the Sea*.

The First Europeans

Our human ancestors, *Homo erectus*, who lived around one million years ago, came to Europe from Africa. It is thought that they crossed the stretch of water between southern Spain and Morocco so it is the Spanish who were the first Europeans. Human fossils and artefacts proving this were found at two sites in Spain –

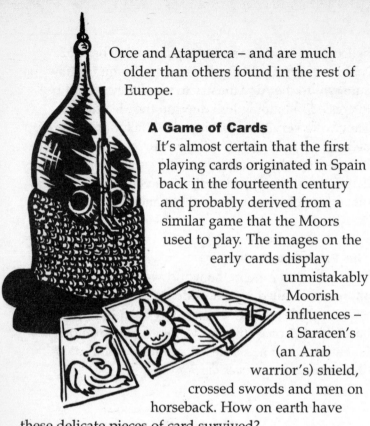

Orce and Atapuerca – and are much older than others found in the rest of Europe.

A Game of Cards

It's almost certain that the first playing cards originated in Spain back in the fourteenth century and probably derived from a similar game that the Moors used to play. The images on the early cards display unmistakably Moorish influences – a Saracen's (an Arab warrior's) shield, crossed swords and men on horseback. How on earth have these delicate pieces of card survived?

Famous Spaniards
Christopher Columbus

Christopher Columbus is probably the world's most famous explorer and the discoverer of the New World – America. He is one of the greatest figures in Spanish history but when you see his name it will be spelt the Spanish way, Cristóbal Colón. Columbus was actually born in Italy but Spain was his adopted country. There is even a national holiday in his honour.

His first voyage at the age of 14 was a disaster. He was shipwrecked and washed up on the coast of Portugal. But he eventually found his way home. Years later, when he dreamt up his famous idea of crossing the Atlantic, he was more experienced and had studied all the latest theories about navigation. People now knew that the world was round, not flat, they knew how to use the stars and the sun to tell them which direction they were going in, and ship design had improved a great deal, making boats sturdier and faster. Everything was now in place for an adventurer to make a truly epic voyage. But it took someone with the courage of Christopher Columbus to take

that first step and put all the theory into practice. He believed that across the ocean was the Indies, where many valuable spices came from and he imagined great wealth, power and prestige if his plan succeeded. However, he needed money to pay for this incredible trip and he did the rounds of the kings and queens of Europe, asking them to help him. Many didn't believe what he said was true, and they declined. Only the King and Queen of Spain agreed to pay for the voyage. They could see that if Columbus was right, he might find unimaginable riches, maybe gold, in the new countries.

In 1492, he set sail with three ships and a large crew from the little town of Palos de la Frontera on the southern coast of Spain. There is a monastery there where Columbus stayed and planned his voyage, and you can visit it to see the spectacular reconstructions of the three ships.

It was two months before they next saw land. Columbus thought it was the Indies – but it was the islands of the Bahamas, just off the coast of America. Columbus didn't know that – how could he? It didn't matter – he'd discovered new land! On his return to Spain, he was honoured and celebrated – his achievement was so great. It's hard to imagine now what it must have been like to set sail and not know what you were going to find. Perhaps the only experience we can compare it to today is when man first stepped on the Moon.

When Columbus died in 1506 in the Spanish city of Valladolid, he remembered how people had made fun

of his idea of sailing across the Atlantic. Nobody was laughing now. He had changed the course of history. The house where he died is no longer there but it has been completely reconstructed and you can visit it. Columbus's tomb is in Seville cathedral. It is quite magnificent – and so it should be!

The Great Conquistadors

After Columbus discovered America, word spread all over Spain and many men wanted to follow in his footsteps. Two great adventurers, **Hernán Cortés** and **Francisco Pizarro** took expeditions to the New World and became known as great conquistadors, conquerors of new territories.

Cortés was born in Medellín in the south of Spain. His father had fought the Moors, so maybe courage and excitement were in the blood! His parents sent him away to study law but he came home determined to live a life of adventure instead.

In 1519, he led an expedition to what is now Mexico – the land of the Aztecs – where the Spaniards thought there would be great treasures, especially gold and

silver. They landed in Veracruz and learnt from the locals that the country was ruled by a great king called Montezuma in a royal city several hundred miles away. The Spanish soldiers wanted to return to Spain, but Cortés persuaded them to stay and they began their long march across Mexico to find Montezuma. When the Aztec king heard the news that they were on their way, he said, 'The gods have come back. Their lances spit fire. The warriors have two heads and six legs and they live in houses that float.'

For many months, the Spanish fought the Aztecs until one day, Cortés dreamt up a daring plan. He took Montezuma prisoner and threatened to kill him if he didn't tell his people to obey Spanish rule. That did it. At last, the conquistador had beaten the mighty Aztec empire.

Back in Spain, news of Cortés's victory spread (how proud his parents must have been!) and Francisco Pizarro, the son of a nobleman, became obsessed with tales of the fabulous wealth belonging to the Incas of Peru. He eventually gained the support of the king and set sail in 1531 with 180 men and 37 horses (an earlier voyage had once set sail without him because Pizarro had injured himself during a romantic tryst).

With even more daring and ruthlessness than Cortés, he managed to capture the Inca king Atahualpa, even though the king had an army of 30,000 Inca soldiers. Peru was now in the hands of the Spanish and Pizarro began to organize his new land. But he was not to remain in charge for long. His recklessness got him into trouble and some of his fellow Spaniards thought he had too much power. Poor old Pizarro was murdered at his dinner table!

It's hard nowadays to justify what the conquistadors did – they took over someone else's country and exploited its people but their bravery was astonishing and the consequences of what they did far-reaching: the Spanish language is now spoken throughout Central and South America, many new foods were brought back to Europe, including peppers, pineapples, potatoes, and chocolate and, for a time, Spain was one of the wealthiest and most powerful countries in the world.

Pablo Picasso
Pablo Picasso was one of the most important artists of the twentieth century. Millions of people have heard of him, have seen his paintings and maybe have a print or two of his pictures hanging on their walls. He achieved worldwide fame and fabulous wealth, something which usually only happens to an artist after their death. Picasso died in 1973 and his paintings are sold

in art auctions for millions of pounds.

He was born in Málaga in 1881 (the house where he was born is now a museum) and began to paint and draw at the age of 10. The pictures he painted as a young man were rather gloomy, often of poor people and circus performers but, as he grew older, he began to paint in a way no one had ever seen before. Until then, painters had tended to portray objects exactly as they were seen, but Picasso began to paint in ways that made objects almost unrecognizable. He might portray a weeping woman by distorting her face, drawing jagged lines across it and using strange colours. He was trying to convey people's emotions and developed a revolutionary new artistic style called Cubism to do this. Once word had spread around the art world, everyone wanted to paint in the same way.

Picasso left Spain and lived in Paris for many years, but many of his paintings and drawings continued to contain images of Spain – guitars and bulls, for example – and one of his most famous paintings, *Guernica*, depicted a terrible scene after the town of Guernica was bombed during Spain's Civil War. The painting does not show the event realistically but uses strange distorted images in black and white to convey the horror of war – a dying horse, a bull, a woman trapped in a burning building, a weeping face. It is one of the most important paintings in the world and made people think a great deal about how terrible it is to be a country at war. You can see it on display at the Reina Sofia art gallery in Madrid. If you want to see more, there is a huge collection of Picasso's paintings, sculptures and pottery in Barcelona's Museu de Picasso. A new Picasso museum opened in Malaga in 2003.

Two Famous Bullfighters

The finest bullfighters in Spain are treated like gods and Juan Belmonte and Joselito were no exception. Joselito first went into the bullring aged 9 and had killed six bulls by the time he was 16. He was the idol of all of Spain and everyone thought he was immortal. But in 1920, when he was 28 years old, he was fatally wounded in a bullfight. It is said that while he was lying on the operating table, he saw a green ball – the gypsy sign of death – hovering over him.

He was succeeded as the idol of Spain by Juan Belmonte, a very small and slim man, who, despite his size, was incredibly brave. He would stand motionless, waiting for the bull to charge, and he got nearer to the bull than anyone else had ever dared. Once Belmonte had done it, everyone had to follow his example and the techniques he used in the ring became commonplace. Unlike Joselito, Belmonte lived to a ripe old age. The bulls never managed to get him!

Salvador Dalí

Salvador Dalí was one of the funniest and most playful artists Spain has ever produced. He was expelled from art school for rebellious behaviour because he claimed he was better than his teachers!

In the 1920s, he became the leader of a group of painters called the Surrealists. They were interested in painting images from the unconscious part of our mind, the part which only reveals itself in our dreams with strange images, frightening scenes and things that don't make sense. So many of their paintings and sculptures are very strange and seem illogical! One of Dalí's most famous paintings is called *The Persistence of Memory* and shows bizarre, melting watches in a very peculiar landscape – something that you might see in your dreams perhaps. It's fun to try and work out what it means but not everybody was amused at the time – many thought that such paintings were terrible and upsetting and shouldn't be exhibited.

Almost everything Dalí did was controversial. He had an outrageous personality and even turned himself into a work of art – he grew a long, curling moustache which made him instantly recognizable and he wore flamboyant, over-the-top clothes. In spite of his eccentricity, everyone wanted Dalí to work for them, so new and exciting was the Surrealist style. He designed jewellery, clothes, stage sets, interiors and even became involved in film-making. He once designed a piece of

Look out for these other famous names in Spain:

☞ **Goya** (1746-1828) a famous painter. One of the greatest figures in Spanish art. You'll see his name everywhere: streets and buildings are named after him, even a Metro station in Madrid.

☞ **Federico García Lorca:** a poet and playwright who died in 1936.

☞ **Félix Lope de Vega:** a sixteenth-century dramatist, a little like Shakespeare.

☞ **Arturo Pérez-Reverte:** a contemporary, bestselling thriller writer. If his latest book is out, you'll see it everywhere.

☞ **Joaquin Cortés:** a young and much-idolized flamenco dancer. He has performed all around the world and is known for performing without his shirt on!

☞ **Penelope Cruz:** she was born in Madrid and appeared many times on Spanish television and in Spanish films before becoming a Hollywood superstar.

☞ **Antonio Banderas:** another Hollywood superstar but he was born in Málaga. He still has a house in Spain and owns a restaurant chain too.

☞ **Jesulín de Ubrique:** a bullfighting god! Tickets to see him perform are very expensive indeed.

☞ **Pedro Almodóvar:** probably Spain's most well-known film director.

jewellery with a ruby heart that was actually beating.

The Dalí Museum, in his hometown of Figueres, is one of the most visited museums in Spain. He designed the museum himself, and it is full of tricks and illusions including a coin-fed car which fills up with water. But the strangest of all is Dalí's tomb – he is actually buried there! How weird is that?

Antonio Gaudí

Gaudí built some of the most unusual and inventive buildings in the world. He was part of an artistic group working in Barcelona called the *Modernistas*, who wanted to break with tradition and design buildings the likes of which no one had ever seen. Very few of Gaudí's creations were built – only the Sagrada Familia church, some houses and apartment buildings and a public park – and all were in his native Barcelona. Despite such a small collection, their impact was enormous because they were unique. The apartment building called the Casa Milá does not have a single straight line, its six storeys appear to be squashed together like cream oozing out of a cake and its strange sculpted chimneys look so spooky that they've been christened 'the witch-scarers'. Parc Güell, a public park built in 1922, shows Gaudí's imagination run wild. It is full of benches (one is the longest in the world) and balconies covered in brightly coloured tiles and sculpted in strange snake-like forms. The park is fabulous, funny and irresistible. Everybody loves it.

It's strange to think that in contrast to his extravagant and imaginative buildings, Gaudí himself was someone who liked to hide away. Unlike his fellow Spaniards, he drank very little wine, didn't go out much, was vegetarian (very unusual in Spain) and usually wore a dark, baggy suit and slippers. It was said that, for some reason, he always told his junior helpers to wear two pairs of socks!

Miguel de Cervantes

Miguel de Cervantes (1547-1616) is the author of one of Spain's greatest novels, *Don Quixote*. Until then, very few people had written novels, just plays and poetry, so this book is extremely important in the history of literature. The book was a hit when it was first published and was read in many other countries as well. Cervantes, who had previously been a soldier before becoming a writer, didn't come up with *Don Quixote* until he was 60 years old.

If you were Spanish, you would probably have to read this at school. It's great fun and tells the story of a hopeless knight called Don Quixote, who roams the Spanish countryside with his companion, Sancho Panza. Don Quixote thinks he's very grand but in reality is poor and rather bad at his job! Cervantes was poking fun at Spanish society through his characters. The images of Don Quixote and Sancho Panza are very well-known throughout Spain and famous artists, including Picasso and Dalí, have painted them.

Two Famous Opera Singers

In the last 50 years, Spain has produced two of the world's finest opera singers – Plácido Domingo and José Carreras (your mum will have heard of them). Both have achieved great fame and fortune from their singing and are known throughout the world. Who'd have thought it when all those years ago, Carreras used to sing to the ladies having their hair done in his mother's hairdressing salon!

Food and Drink

I n Spain, eating and
drinking is a national
pastime and a great
deal of family and social
life takes place around the
dinner table or in the local cafés
and bars. Spain has more restaurants and cafés than
any other country in the world, and they are usually
crowded and very lively when everyone comes out to
eat.

Most cafés will have a bar, where alcohol is served,
but children are always allowed inside. In fact, you'll
be positively welcomed but you won't find a special
children's menu or a particular part of the café where
you have to sit – everyone eats the same things and
everyone eats together.

In many places, the television (usually mounted on
the wall) will probably be on – no one wants to miss
the football! You'll also notice lots of sausages and
cured meats dangling from hooks, maybe a huge
haunch of ham or two. One other thing – don't be
surprised to see people throw their used serviettes and
toothpicks straight onto the floor. In fact, it's

considered rude to leave them on the counter, so go ahead and drop them – nobody will mind.

The Spanish eating schedule is very different from ours and can take some getting used to, especially the timing of the evening meal. It goes something like this:

Breakfast – children tend to have a milky chocolate drink called *cola-cao*, which can be bought in all the supermarkets. This is usually had with little pieces of plain, sweet cake (they come in all shapes and sizes). Adults will have coffee and a pastry (perhaps) or a *tostada* (toasted crispy roll with butter and jam).

Mid-morning snack – it is common for people to take a short break from their work to go and have something sweet, or a *bocadillo* (a roll with cheese or meat inside) and coffee in the nearest café. Spain is a nation of coffee-drinkers and everywhere, even in the most remote village, you will find a café or bar that serves coffee (the Spanish don't like tea and if you ask them to make you a cuppa – yuck!).

Lunch (around 2 o'clock) – everything comes to a halt as everyone either heads home to eat or visits a favourite café or restaurant for lunch. Lunch, which is often three courses, might (if you're at home) be followed by a siesta. This is a short nap, not so much to sleep off the effects of a hefty lunch as to escape the extreme heat at the hottest part of the day. Many shops and businesses will close from 1 o'clock until 4 o'clock.

Merienda-time (around 5 o'clock) – this snack will keep you going until the evening meal.

Evening *tapas* (8 to 10 o'clock) – *tapas* are small portions of food or appetizers. Spanish people often meet up to eat *tapas* while having a drink, regardless of whether they're going to eat their evening meal together or not. The selection of *tapas* varies from café to café and it's fun to move around and try as many as you can – they provide an opportunity to sample some of the most popular staple foods in Spain. A basic selection will probably consist of a plate of crisps, a dish of olives, a slice of *tortilla* (delicious potato omelette), a selection of meats and sausages, meat and fish croquettes, a small portion of a chicken (or lamb stew) and some bread.

Evening meal (10 to 11 o'clock) – it's been a long wait and, if you've tried to find somewhere to eat any earlier, you'll either have found it was closed or you'll have had a meal in an empty restaurant, just you and the waiter!

In Spain, geography and history have influenced the food that is grown locally and the way it is cooked. The country is so mountainous and hot that it is difficult to raise cattle because there simply isn't enough green grass for them to eat, so Spain is not noted for its beef dishes and dairy products. But the land is fertile enough for farming smaller animals, such as chickens, sheep and pigs, and it is perfect for growing olives and grapes. Eggs, lamb, pork and ham are eaten all over Spain; olive oil is used as the basis for cooking; wine (for grown-ups only, of course) washes it all down.

Spain has the longest coastline in Europe with plenty of fish, and not just in the coastal regions. Inland, the demand for fresh fish is high, and catches of the day are rushed overnight in refrigerated lorries to reach the city markets first thing in the morning.

If you're vegetarian, finding a daily variety of things to eat might be difficult, but among these you are likely to taste one or more of the foods the Spanish brought back to Europe from the New World, including

peppers, potatoes, sweetcorn, tomatoes and chocolate. Many Spanish dishes are cooked to recipes hundreds of years old, passed down from generation to generation and many show an Arab influence from the time the Moors ruled Spain.

The Spanish are extremely proud of their food and with good reason – it's absolutely delicious! A good deal of the wonderful flavour comes from the fresh ingredients used. There are few ready-prepared meals and most dishes are cooked from scratch. In addition to large supermarkets, there are smaller specialist food shops in towns and cities, but the most exciting way to buy fresh food in Spain is to visit one of the many markets, some of which are housed in beautiful old buildings. The market in Santander has the most amazing variety of fish and Valencia market has more than 1,000 stalls under the same roof (incidentally, it has a lovely parrot and swordfish weathervane on the the top). But La Boquería market in Barcelona must be one of Europe's most spectacular food markets. There is a bewildering variety of fruit, vegetables, fish and meat for sale, all beautifully displayed, and the market women proudly wear their frilly white embroidered pinafores. In La Boquería, you will see all of the foods of Spain. You can't fail to be impressed.

Here are some classic Spanish dishes that you're bound to come across:

☞ Cured sausages and meats, especially ham (*jamón*) – there is a huge variety to choose from but the most popular is *chorizo*, a reddish-coloured sausage flavoured with spices – you'll see it everywhere. In Asturias, where the winters can be damp and chilly, the famous local dish is *fabada*, a wonderful, warming stew of sausage, cured meat and beans.

☞ *Cocido* – a meat and vegetable stew, whose recipe changes from region to region.

☞ Chicken, pork, lamb and veal, often plain, fried in olive oil and served with chips. In the Castile region, there are many restaurants that serve traditional suckling pig (baby pigs roasted in huge ovens). In Sepúlveda, near Segovia, whole lambs are roasted instead. The region is so famous for this way of cooking that it is known as *España del Asado* (Spain of the Roast).

☞ *Pinchitos morunos* – little kebabs of chicken or pork, flavoured with spices.

☞ *Empanada* – a speciality of Galicia, these are pies stuffed with meat or fish.

☞ Barbecued sardines – you'll see people snacking on these at the beach in the summer. Very tasty.

☞ *Patatas bravas* – fried potatoes in a delicious spicy sauce. In Madrid, there's even a café that specializes in preparing *patatas* and different sauces.

Paella – the dish everyone has heard of! It is eaten all over Spain but the classic *paella* comes from Valencia and consists of chicken, *chorizo*, ham, shrimp, lobster, clams, mussels, peas, onion, peppers, rice and saffron (the most expensive spice in the world – it gives the rice its yellow colour) and is served in a flat pan from which the dish takes its name. Valencia became the rice-growing region of Spain when the Romans first irrigated the land and the Arabs then perfected the system.

☞ *Gazpacho* soup – a refreshing, chilled vegetable soup, originally from the hottest part of Spain, Andalucía.

☞ *Pimientos de Padrón* – these deep-fried peppers are served with salt. They are so tiny that 20 make up a portion. Every now and then, you'll bite into a fiery, hot one.

☞ *Churros* – at every fiesta, you are sure to find a cauldron of bubbling oil in which these fritters are cooked. They taste like doughnuts and are often eaten dipped in hot chocolate.

☞ *Crema catalana* – a creamy, sweet custard with a golden brown top layer of caramelized sugar.

☞ Oranges, lemons, melons, figs, strawberries, cherries, peaches and pomegranates are mostly grown in the south. If you're in Valencia, you might catch on the breeze the scent of oranges from the orange tree groves!

☞ *Turrón* – a delicious nougat made from almonds, sugar and honey, usually eaten at Christmas but available all year round. You can buy soft or hard versions, with nuts or covered in chocolate.

☞ *Horchata* – a speciality of Valencia, this thirst-quenching, milky drink made from nuts can be found in other Spanish regions as well. It is served chilled and is sometimes drunk with sweet biscuits.

By the way, apart from *Horchata*, you'll find the same drinks in Spain that you'll find at home: cola, lemonade, mineral water and fruit juices.

These are some of the more unusual dishes:

☞ *Angulas* – tiny baby eels as thin as beansprouts that are caught and plunged straight into boiling water into which (so they say) a piece of cigar has been added for flavour.

☞ *Pulpo* – octopus looks very strange and slimy before it's cooked but is actually quite tasty.

☞ *Percebes* – extremely expensive, very ugly, rare barnacles from Galicia, often sold while still stuck to the rock. The King of all Seafood, they say…

☞ *Yemas* (candied egg yolks) – these bright yellow sweets made from egg yolks, sugar, lemon and cinnamon are traditionally made by nuns from a 400-year-old recipe. Many Spanish biscuits and sweets originated centuries ago in convents, where they were prepared as treats for Easter and Christmas. You can sometimes spot price lists of sweet things pinned on convent doors.

Festivals and National Celebrations

The Spanish love to get together and celebrate. All festivities take place with a lot of noise and energy. There are several national and regional holidays, usually with a religious connection, held either in honour of an important saint or a key date in the Christian calendar, such as Easter or Corpus Christi (in memory of Christ's Last Supper). But even though the reason for celebration is often religious, it doesn't mean to say that the mood is serious. Far from it! It's really fun to go to *fiestas*, where there are always eating, drinking, dancing and fireworks – the party is for everyone, from babies to grannies.

Just like everybody else all over the world, the major festive occasions, such as Easter, Christmas and New Year, are traditionally spent with the family but the Spanish do also like to celebrate outdoors with strangers. You really can't be shy and retiring in Spain!

¡Feliz Navidad! (Merry Christmas!)
¡Feliz Año Nuevo! (Happy New Year!)

If you're in Spain during Christmas or New Year, you'll soon realize that this country has its own special ways of celebrating this time of year. In most of northern Europe, 25 December is the day everybody looks forward to, when presents are exchanged and the Christmas meal is eaten, but in Spain the really important day of the festive season is 6 January, known as *Día de Reyes* (Kings' Day), when the Magi arrived in Bethlehem with gifts for the infant Jesus. It's not Father Christmas who brings presents to Spanish children, but the Three Kings.

In Great Britain, 6 January is Twelfth Night, traditionally the day when the Christmas festivities come to an end. Just as we're taking down the Christmas tree, the decorations and getting ready to go back to school, the Spanish are beginning to get into the swing of things!

Christmas Eve and Christmas Day are still important celebrations in Spain, and families get together on Christmas Eve for a huge meal. They then go to church for Midnight Mass, but don't be surprised if, on

Christmas Day, you see some people at work, usually in bars or restaurants. There is some gift-giving on Christmas Day, often a present of money called the *aguinaldo*, which grandparents give to their grandchildren.

On New Year's Eve, Spanish children prepare for the midnight eating of the 12 lucky grapes! In Madrid, crowds gather in one of the main squares and, as the clock strikes 12, you are supposed to swallow a grape for each of the chimes. If you finish before or on the last chime, you will have good luck in the coming year. The Madrid celebrations are televised yearly so people can follow the event from home as well.

When 6 January finally comes around, everyone can receive their presents, but not before the Three Kings' Parade has been held, which takes place the day before in many town and city squares. In some coastal towns, the Three Kings arrive by boat! Huge crowds gather and the Kings throw sweets into the crowd. Children leave their shoes outside for the Kings to put presents in, taking great care not to forget a bunch of carrots and some water for the camels.

Easter

Easter is called *Semana Santa* (Holy Week). Of all Spain's celebrations, *Semana Santa* is the most solemn. Almost every town or village holds processions and gatherings over the holiday week. The most spectacular of these takes place in Seville and people from all over the country and from around the world, come to watch the amazing events. There are about 100 churches in Seville and every church (in fact, every church in Spain) has statues of Jesus and the Virgin Mary. These images are often incredibly elaborate and extremely heavy. It can take up to 40 men to carry one statue. The statues are paraded through the streets of Seville towards the cathedral, where the procession stops and returns to the church from where it started, followed by hundreds of people. A band sometimes accompanies the procession. During this festival, you will be amazed at what you see: followers walking barefoot and carrying enormous crosses on their backs, or others dressed in spooky-looking white hoods (with holes cut out for the eyes) and capes. The crowds are huge and people get very emotional when the most famous statue (that of the Virgin Mary

with tears falling down her cheeks) is paraded through the streets. Listen out for the lovely, mournful singing that often accompanies the processions.

If this is all too much, or seems too strange, you can always go searching for the special Easter sweets and decorated cakes that are on sale, although you'll find very few chocolate eggs and Easter bunnies!

Fiestas

What Spain really excels at – and no other country can beat it at this – is putting body and soul into its *fiestas*. These local celebrations are held in cities, towns and villages all over the country. There are hundreds of them – almost any day of the year, there will be a *fiesta* in full swing. And they are all, without exception, extremely noisy. There isn't a village, town or city that doesn't honour its patron saint or the changing seasons with a huge bash. In the wine-making regions, for instance, the end of the grape harvest is a great reason to hold a *fiesta*. Some are spectacular and draw crowds from miles around; some are small and very local but just as treasured by those who attend them. If you happen to be staying somewhere that is holding its *fiesta*, don't even think about trying to get a good night's sleep – just relax, join in, let off steam and celebrate!

Some Spectacular Fiestas
Carnival (everywhere in February or early March)
Held in many towns and villages all over Spain, this is a chance to throw a party and have fun before Lent when everyone must fast. It's a great excuse to wear fancy dress. One of the best carnivals is in Cádiz – the whole city dresses up and sings songs that poke fun at local figures, pop stars and other celebrities. Carnival ends just before Easter with a very funny ritual called the Burial of the Sardine. A pretend sardine is burned or buried to represent the end of winter. No one takes anything too seriously!

***Las Fallas* in Valencia (19 March)**
During this celebration, huge papier-mâché figures (*fallas*) are put on display in the squares of Valencia. The figures are usually of politicians and celebrities, take months to build and the city comes alive with the sound of fireworks and the noisy burning of these paper statues. At this time of year – the beginning of spring – it is traditional to light bonfires to celebrate the end of winter, but this particular *fiesta* began when Valencia's workers would burn the wooden poles on

which their lamps rested during the winter. Spring had arrived!

Every day of the *fiesta*, you can walk through Valencia's squares and inspect the statues as you eat your *churros* and chocolate. There is a prize for the best statue and on 19 March, when they are all set alight, only the winner will be saved from the flames and kept in the local museum.

Los Sanfermines in Pamplona (7–14 July)

Every morning of this *fiesta* at 8 o'clock, six bulls are released to run wild through the cobbled streets of the old town. Hundreds of men wearing traditional white shirts, red sashes and neckerchiefs try their luck and run alongside or in front of the bulls, shouting and yelling. Every year, many people are injured: it's an extremely dangerous thing to do even though the race lasts no longer than three

minutes. The Pamplona streets twist and turn and the angry bulls run at incredible speeds. Their final destination is the bullring, where they will then be rounded up to await their turn in the ring when the bullfighting begins later in the day. If you're not in Pamplona that week, you can watch the race through the streets live on national television – while eating your breakfast!

The bull-running is the highlight of the *fiesta*, but there are plenty of other things to do so long as you don't mind being woken up at a quarter to seven in the morning by a noisy band eager to get everyone out of bed. There are fireworks (of course), dancing, giant figure processions, men wearing cardboard horses around their waists and more races around the streets (without bulls). On the last day, everything comes to an end with a candlelit procession and everyone singing, 'Poor me! Another *Los Sanfermines* has ended'.

Moors and Christians in Alcoi, near Alicante (April)

To commemorate Spain winning back the country from the Moors, Alcoi holds a magnificent procession in which everyone dresses up either as a Moor or a Christian and then goes into mock battle. A wooden fortress is put up in the main square

and the armies all meet up there. It is the most incredible sight – Christian soldiers in armour; the Moors in white cloaks, turbans and feathered headdresses; in the background, fireworks, a band and cheering crowds. There are several re-enactments like this throughout the region at this time of year, but the battle at Alcoi is the biggest and the best. The rest of the year, it's a sleepy little town!

San Isidro in Madrid (15 May)

Madrid likes to throw a party in honour of St Isidro, the city's patron saint! There are concerts, processions and many people wear traditional dress. The women look especially fine wearing brightly coloured flamenco dresses and beautifully embroidered fringed shawls. You can buy the shawls in many of the city's shops, along with decorated fans, which are extremely useful for cooling yourself down in the hot weather.

All week, Madrid holds spectacular bullfights (*corridas*), which thousands of people flock to see. Bullfights are often held at *fiesta* time and, although there are only a few hundred or so held every year, the *corridas* play a crucial part in Spanish life. The fights are shown live on television and the passion of the spectators has to be seen to be believed. Famous bullfighters are mobbed wherever they go and their lives followed closely in the gossip magazines. Just like popstars really.

Tickets to the *corrida* can be expensive, especially if well-known *matadors* (bull-fighters) are performing and if you want to sit in the shade (the heat of the full sun can be unbearable). Bullfights take place in the evening when the sun is not quite so hot, but this is Spain and it's still very warm even at seven o'clock at night. Outside the bullring, you can buy souvenirs – posters, models of bulls and little *matador* dolls and hear the roar of the crowd.

As bull-fighting can be a dangerous activity, a bullring will have a small chapel where the bullfighters pray for success and a mini-infirmary, where they can be patched up if things haven't gone well! There are also stables and dressing rooms. Other famous bullrings are at Seville, Ronda, Málaga and Cádiz. They all hold bullfights at *fiesta* time.

The *Romería del Rocío* at El Rocío (May/June)

This *fiesta* is ancient and attracts people from all over Spain (nearly one million come to take part)! Over the course of a weekend, they travel to the little village of El Rocío in Andalusia. They come on foot, horseback or in painted wagons. Women often dress in traditional flamenco dress, the men wear old-fashioned short jackets and everyone celebrates on the way. The focus of the *fiesta* is a famous statue of the Virgin Mary and the highlight of the proceedings is the carrying of the statue around the village and then taking it back to its chapel. It's an extraordinary sight, so many people in such a small place, and the presence of horses and traditional costume are very typical of this part of Spain. Many Andalusian towns and villages hold horse displays as part of their *fiesta*, where horsemen demonstrate their riding skills. There is a famous horse celebration at Jeréz de la Frontera in May – not to be missed if you're in that part of Spain.

A Little Bit of Sport

Fútbol

Fútbol (football) is the most popular sport in Spain. Millions of people watch it and there are many television and radio programmes, newspapers and magazines devoted to it. The top five teams in Spain are Real Madrid, Barcelona, Valencia, Athletic Bilbao, RC Deportivo and Atlético Madrid. There is fierce rivalry between the two richest and most successful clubs – Real Madrid and Barcelona.

If you want to know who's playing where and when, look it up in the daily sports newspaper called *La Marca*. Matches are usually played on a Sunday, and occasionally on a Saturday, to make televising them more convenient. It's not expensive or difficult to get tickets. A really good ticket for a top game, say

---

Facts about Real Madrid

☞ Founded in 1902. Acquired the 'Real' (Royal) in 1932, given by King Alfonso XIII.

☞ Stadium = Santiago Bernabéu

☞ Colours = white

☞ Real Madrid was the first team to win the European Cup in 1956 and has since then won it a further eight times. The fans are very demanding – when the team wasn't doing so well in 1999, they threatened the club's highly paid players with: 'We will burn your Ferraris!' Some of the world's superstar players play for this club, including Figo, Zidane, Ronaldo and David Beckham.

---

between Real Madrid and Barcelona or for the equivalent of the FA Cup – the *Copa del Rey* – will be hard to come by, but that's to be expected. Tickets go on sale one week before the match, with club members first in the pecking order. Then three or four days before the game, anyone can buy them.

The atmosphere at a football match is generally very good-natured and there's no violence. Whole families attend the game, often bringing very young children with them. Buy a bag of *pipas* (sunflower seeds) to nibble. They are quite tricky to eat! The day after the match, the programme to watch is *El Día Despúes* (translated, this means The Day

After). It's fronted by an
Englishman called Michael
Robinson who has
been involved in
Spanish football
for many years.
He's very
popular,
very funny
and still
speaks
Spanish
with an
English accent.

If you can't make it to a live match, then catch it on
the radio, where there are masses of sports programmes,
many of them broadcasting live matches. Or you could
go and find a café and play table football. Everybody
plays *futbolín* (table football) and anyone will give you a
game.

Cycling

Second only to football in terms of popularity, this is
the serious, Tour de France kind of cycling. There are
cycling clubs in most Spanish cities and towns. If
you're in the countryside, especially in a mountainous
area, you'll see groups of cyclists everywhere, up at the
crack of dawn to beat the heat on their way up the
mountains. In addition to the Tour de France, in which
Spanish cyclists play a major part (Miguel Induraín

won the Tour de France five times!), there are four important cycle races in Spain, each one followed with great passion. They are all extremely challenging, especially the three-week-long *Vuelta a España* (Tour of Spain), which begins in the highest village in Spain, Trevélez, and takes the cyclists up the highest mainland mountain, Mulhacén, at 3,481 metres (11,426 feet)! The *Vuelta* is a huge event with people lining the course to cheer on the cyclists, who are considered to be truly great sportsmen, showing tremendous endurance, strength and discipline. You can't argue with that!

Other sports

Some of the best surfing waters in Europe are in Spain: in Tarifa on the south coast, along the Bay of Biscay and in Galicia – in fact, almost anywhere on the ferocious Atlantic coast. Skiing, golf, tennis and basketball (it's played at school and is very popular) are all followed with great enthusiasm in Spain, but they don't attract the crowds in quite the same way as football or cycling do.

The only traditional game played to any great extent is *pelota*. This is a sport from the Basque country and in the Basque language is called *Jai-Alai*, which means 'merry festival'. This is a reference to the fact that it was first played way back in the fifteenth century at religious and holiday festivals, often against church walls. *Pelota* is a game with eight players. The players stand in a line and serve the ball (a tough little rubber ball, harder than a golf ball) against a wall. The second player in the line must catch the ball and serve again for the next player to catch. Players use a long leather glove with a scoop at the end to serve and catch. It's called a *cesta*. If you miss the ball then you must go to the end of the line and wait your turn again. The first player to win seven points is the winner. It's a very fast and furious game and the *Guinness Book of Records* has confirmed that the fastest serve in the world was a *pelota* serve. Players must wear protective headgear – it's a little dangerous but very exciting to watch! There's a league and a championship, too.

Sometimes you might

see players using a *cesta* made from woven material, not leather. The story behind this concerns a young player who couldn't afford the leather *cesta* so he tried hurling the ball with the basket from his mother's kitchen. It worked – and it caught on!

The Basques have cornered the market in unusual sports. They also have competitions involving tests of strength, such as log-splitting and weight-lifting. There is also a famous rowing boat race around the bay at San Sebastián.

If you don't fancy taking up any of these sports, then you should just settle for the gentle game of *palas*. On every beach in Spain, you will see people playing this. With a round wooden bat the size of a tennis racquet, you have to hit a ball to your fellow player, backwards and forwards. The aim is to see how long you can keep it in the air. It's not as easy as it sounds!

Fiestas and Unusual Customs

Spain is such a traditional country and it honours and keeps many of its old customs. Some are strange and some are *very* strange. But, as with the more popular and well-established *fiestas*, nothing is taken too seriously and there's always an excuse for a party.

La Tomatina in Buñol (last Wednesday in August)

Put on your scruffiest clothes because this fiesta is messy! At 11 o'clock in the morning, lorryloads of ripe tomatoes are driven slowly through the streets and everyone grabs handfuls and hurls them at each other in a mad tomato war. They shout '¡*Tomate! ¡Tomate!*' and get hosed down later by the local fire brigade. Nobody quite knows how *La Tomatina* began. Some say it was a fight between friends. Others say it started when rebellious locals hurled tomatoes at the town officials.

Human Castles in Tarragona and Catalonia (last week of September/early October)

The crowd is very quiet as teams of men stand on each other's shoulders, building a human tower as high as they can go. The Catalans have been building human castles all over the region for centuries and records show that nine storeys of three or four people have been achieved. The most difficult is the tower of one person per storey, called a *pilar*. The highest *pilar* was eight storeys high! The castle is only complete when a small child scrambles up and stands on the top. Then and only then does the crowd burst into very loud applause and cheering. If everyone can dismantle themselves without falling down, then so much the better!

Os Peliqueiros in Ourense (February or March)

Men dress up in extraordinary costumes with masks and huge hats and walk along the streets lashing out at the crowds with sticks. There is also a battle with flour, water and live ants as ammunition. Shout and scream – it's allowed!

The Matchmaker in Madrid

(13 June)

On this day at the church of San
Antonio de la Florida, unmarried
women take 13 pins and place them in
the font inside the church. They then
pray for the saint to bring them a
husband. The queues can be very long,
snaking all the way around the block.

The *Sardana*

This is Catalonia's national dance and is
performed at many fiestas. The dancers
form a circle and everyone jumps and
skips in a series of very complicated
moves. Everybody looks terribly serious as they
concentrate on the dance. A band accompanies them to
liven up the proceedings.

Firewalking in San Pedro Manrique

(23 June)

This needs to be seen to be believed. Men walk over
burning embers, sometimes carrrying people on their
shoulders. It is said that only the people from that
village can walk away without burning their feet!

La Folía in San Vicente de la Barquera (April)

In this town, the statue of the Virgin Mary was said to

have mysteriously arrived in a boat with no crew and no sails. So, once a year, it is taken out to sea on a beautifully decorated fishing boat, with a grand *flotilla* of the rest of the town's boats following behind.

El Colacho in Castrillo de Murcia (May or June)

In this village, all babies born during the previous year are dressed in their Sunday best and laid down on mattresses on the street. *El Colacho*, a man dressed in a red and yellow costume said to represent the Devil, jumps over them to cure them of any illnesses. The parents watch with worried looks on their faces!

A Rapa das Bestas in Galicia (over the summer months)

All around Galicia's coast there are semi-wild horses roaming the pastures. During the summer, they are all rounded up and their manes and tails are cut. The horses are a splendid sight to see and usually the rounding-up turns into a *fiesta*. Expect music and dancing – and fireworks, of course.

Santa María de Ribarteme (29 July)

This day marks the occasion for a pilgrimage made in coffins by people who narrowly escaped death the year before!

Odds and Ends

Hot and Cold, High and Low

Spain is a hot country and many people are astonished when you tell them that you can go skiing in several different places. It's even more astonishing when you realize that from several points in the very south of the country, you can catch a glimpse of Africa, just across the water from Cádiz. In the springtime, you can go skiiing in the Sierra Nevada mountains in Southern Spain, and catch a glimpse of the Atlas Mountains in Morocco while you're up there, then hop in the car and in an hour's time be swimming in the Mediterranean Sea. How's that for variety? But, you can only do that as winter is drawing to a close, no other time of year will do.

Storks

In villages and towns all over Spain, but especially in the south, you can see storks' nests on top of roofs, towers, spires and chimney pots. They are a funny sight if you've never seen one before because the nests are so huge,

built from branches and twigs and lined with grass. The storks sit on top, surveying the scene, waiting for their eggs to hatch. The birds come from Africa to spend the summer in Spain, then fly south again for the winter. In 1997, one tiny village found itself virtually under siege when 534 storks came to stay that summer. They're noisy, too. You'll probably hear them before you see them.

Bulls

Bred in the fields north of Madrid, bulls provide a truly original solution to the problem of prison security. The main prison of the Madrid area is surrounded by these fields and any prisoner brave or foolish enough to escape has a most terrifying enemy to outwit before he can reach the open road.

Harry Potter in Spanish

☞ *Harry Potter and the Philosopher's Stone (Harry Potter y la Piedra Filosofal)*

☞ *Harry Potter and the Chamber of Secrets (Harry Potter y la Cámara Secreta)*

☞ *Harry Potter and the Prisoner of Azkaban (Harry Potter y el Prisionero de Azkaban)*

☞ *Harry Potter and the Goblet of Fire (Harry Potter y el Cáliz de Fuego)*

☞ Harry Potter and the Order of the Phoenix *(Harry Potter y la Orden del Fénix)*

Some other books you might recognize:

☞ *The Hobbit (El Hobbit)*

☞ *The Lord of the Rings (El Señor de los Anillos)*

☞ *Charlie and the Chocolate Factory (Charlie y la Fábrica de Chocolate)*

☞ *The Lion, the Witch and the Wardrobe (El León, La Bruja y el Ropero)*

The Lottery

The first-ever lotteries were held in Spain in 1763 and have been going strong ever since. There are two different lotteries: the state-run lottery and the lottery run by the charity for the blind. You'll often see blind people in the street selling tickets. They have special permission to do so.

The Christmas lottery *El Gordo* (The Fat One) is a huge occasion and tickets cost about £30 each, but the payout is massive. There is a Spanish superstition that 'bad luck never comes without a reason' and many people hope that the reason is winning the lottery! Therefore some people will travel to a town or village that has seen misfortune – some flooding perhaps – to buy their ticket.

I-Spy Alexander Fleming

Almost every town and city in Spain has a street named after Alexander Fleming, the Scottish scientist who discovered penicillin in 1928. There are also many statues of this man, several hospital wings and medical schools in his name and, until recently, in Barcelona there was an annual ceremony of laying flowers by the memorial erected in his honour. It's hard to think of another non-Spaniard who is celebrated in this way. He's probably the only Scottish person the Spanish will have heard of!

Fleming's great discovery changed the face of medicine and everyone experienced the benefits – so many diseases which once were fatal could now be cured. Fleming became a worldwide celebrity but Spain, in particular, took him to their hearts. He visited Spain and was mobbed by crowds of grateful Spaniards, especially the firemen and the *matadors* of Seville and Barcelona (thankful that many of their bullfighting injuries could now be healed), who knelt down before him. Look out for the streets named after him. *Calle Dr Fleming* (Dr Fleming Street). Play I-Spy, you're sure to find one.

Tío Pepe

If you're in Madrid and you visit Puerta del Sol – which you're bound to because it's in the very centre – then you can't fail to notice the huge *Tío Pepe* (Uncle Joe) advertising sign on top of one of the buildings – it's very famous. *Tío Pepe* is a sherry!

Chupa Chups® – Dalí's Lollipop

The striped logo on the *Chupa Chups®* wrapper was designed by Salvador Dalí and, apart from some very slight changes over the years, it is just the same as the 1958 original. Dalí drew a draft of the design on the back of a newspaper and, within an hour, the finished logo was ready. He had been asked to do this by Enric Bernat, a sweet salesman, who invented *Chupa Chups®* when he noticed that sweets made children's hands sticky. He stuck a sweet on a stick and built a huge business empire around this simple idea. *Chupa Chups®* are sold worldwide, even in Russia and China, and were taken on the 1995 space shuttle! By the way, in case you were wondering, *Chupa Chups®* means 'Sucky Sucks'!

Mercedes Benz

Everyone has heard of the Mercedes Benz, the very swanky German motorcar, but very few people know how it got its name. The car's designer, Herr Benz, married a Spanish woman and they had a child called Mercedes, which is a popular Spanish name. Herr Benz decided to name his beautiful car after his beautiful daughter...

Big Black Bulls

If you happen to be zooming along Spanish motorways, you are bound to see one of the famous Osborne black bulls standing prominently by the road, often on top of a small hill. These are enormous bull silhouettes made of metal and held up by scaffolding, and the first time you see one, you'll be amazed at how big they are (they weigh 50 tonnes!). Originally, they bore the logo of Osborne, a sherry and brandy company, but the logos were removed, so as not to distract drivers, and now they stand, silent and wordless, and seem to fit perfectly into the Spanish landscape. There are over 100 of them throughout Spain. Keep your eyes on the horizon or you'll miss one!

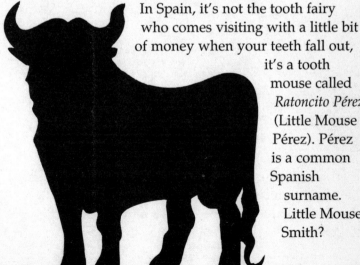

The Tooth Mouse

In Spain, it's not the tooth fairy who comes visiting with a little bit of money when your teeth fall out, it's a tooth mouse called *Ratoncito Pérez* (Little Mouse Pérez). Pérez is a common Spanish surname. Little Mouse Smith?

A Ghost Story

In 1971, in the village of Belmez in southern Spain, a woman was cooking supper when her grandchild pointed to the ground. Staring up from the tiles covering the floor was a face. The woman scrubbed the floor (even had it taken up and replaced with concrete) but the faces kept appearing – for the next two years. Eventually, after some investigation, it was revealed that the house had been built on the site of an old graveyard. Did that have something to do with it?

Emergency
Phrases

Hello/Goodbye	*¡Hola! ¡Adiós!*
Good morning	*Buenos días*
Good evening	*Buenas noches*
Yes/No	*Sí/No*
Please	*Por favor*
Thank you	*Gracias*
Okay	*Vale*
Excuse me	*Perdón*
I'm sorry	*Lo siento*
That's fine	*Está bien*
What…?	*¿Qué…?*
Who…?	*¿Quién…?*
When…?	*¿Cuándo…?*
Why…?	*¿Por qué…?*
How…?	*¿Cómo…?*
My name is…	*Me llamo…*
I don't know.	*No sé.*
Do you speak English?	*¿Habla inglés?*
Does anyone speak English?	*¿Hay alguien que habla inglés?*
I am English.	*Soy inglés/inglesa.*
I'm lost.	*Me he perdido/a*
(*perdido* if you're a boy/*perdida* if you're a girl).	
Can you help me?	*¿Puede usted ayudarme?*
Help!	*¡Socorro!*
Go away!	*¡Váyase!*

I don't understand.	*No entiendo.*
I understand.	*Entiendo.*
Could you speak more slowly, please?	*¿Puede hablar más despacio por favor?*
Could you write that down, please?	*¿Puede escribirlo por favor?*
I don't understand Spanish.	*No entiendo español.*
I only speak a little Spanish.	*Sólo hablo un poco de español.*
Which is the way out?	*¿Dónde está la salida?*
Where are the toilets?	*¿Dónde están los servicios?*

Getting Around

near	*cerca*
far	*lejos*
Turn left	*Gire a la izquierda*
Turn right	*Gire a la derecha*
here/there	*aquí/allí*
I want to go to…	*Quiero ir a…*
I'm looking for…	*Estoy buscando…*
I'm looking for my hotel.	*Estoy buscando mi hotel.*
Where is…?	*¿Dónde está…?*
the Underground	*el metro*
the city centre	*el centro de la ciudad*
street	*la calle*
my hotel	*mi hotel*

the toilets	*los servicios/los aseos*
the Internet café	*el Cibercafé*
the football stadium	*el estadio de fútbol*
the market	*el mercado*
the post office	*Correos*
the beach	*la playa*
the sea	*el mar*
the castle	*el castillo*
the museum	*el museo*
the cathedral	*la catedral*
the church	*la iglesia*
the main square	*la plaza mayor*
the palace	*el palacio*
What time does it open?	*¿A qué hora abren?*
What time does it close?	*¿A qué hora cierran?*

Shopping

How much is it?	*¿Cuánto cuesta?*
Could I have a stamp for the United Kingdom?	*¿Me puede dar un sello para el Reino Unido?*
Do you have…?	*¿Tiene…?*
Do you have any comics?	*¿Tiene tebeos?*
I'm just looking, thank you.	*Sólo estoy mirando, gracias.*
This one.	*Éste.*
That one.	*Ése.*

sale	*la rebaja*
Changing rooms	*Los probadores (in shops)/ el vestuario (sports)*
Pay here	*Pague aquí.*
the bakery	*la panadería*
the cake shop	*la pastelería*
the newspaper stand	*el kiosko de prensa*
the chemist's	*la farmacia*
the bookshop	*la librería*
the greengrocer's	*la frutería*
the shoe shop	*la zapatería*
the supermarket	*el supermercado*
the record shop	*la tienda de discos*
the fishmonger's	*la pescadería*

Food and Drink

breakfast	*el desayuno*
lunch	*el almuerzo/la comida*
dinner	*la cena*
a knife	*un cuchillo*
a fork	*un tenedor*
a spoon	*una cuchara*
a glass	*un vaso*
a bottle	*una botella*
Not for me, thank you	*Para mí no, gracias.*

I'm full!	*Estoy lleno/a* *(lleno* if you're a boy, *llena* if you're a girl).
This octopus is delicious!	*¡El pulpo está delicioso!*
Could I have some chips with this, please?	*Me puede dar papas fritas con esto, por favor?*
It is very tasty.	*Sabe muy bien.*
I would like a …	*Me gustaría un/una …*
Coke	*la Coca-Cola*
a fizzy mineral water	*un agua mineral con gas*
a still mineral water	*un agua mineral sin gas*
an orange juice	*un jugo de naranja*
an ice cream	*un helado*
some *churros* and drinking chocolate	*churros y chocolate*
I am vegetarian	*Soy vegetariano/a* *(vegetariano* if you're a boy, *vegetariana* if you're a girl)

The Menu

Starters	*Entremeses*
Fish	*Pescado*
Meat and poultry	*Carnes y aves*
Vegetables	*Verduras y legumbres*
Fruit	*Frutas*
Desserts	*Postres*
Drinks	*Bebidas*

Health

I'm asthmatic/epileptic/ diabetic	*Soy asmático/a/epiléptico/a/ diabético/a*
I'm allergic to antibiotics/ penicillin/nuts/ fish/cats/birds	*Soy alérgico/a a los antibióticos/ a la penicilina/a las nueces/ al pescado/a los gatos/a los pájaros.*
I am ill.	*No me siento bien.*
I think I'm going to be sick.	*Siento que voy a vomitar.*
I've been stung.	*Me han picado.*

Sport

Who's playing in this match?	*¿Quién esta jugando este partido?*
What team do you support?	*¿De qué equipo eres?*
Who's winning?	*¿Quién está ganando?*
Have you got table football?	*¿Tienen futbolín?*
Can I play table football?	*¿Puedo jugar al futbolín?*
Have you got PlayStation™?	*¿Tiene PlayStation™?*
I'd like to hire a bicycle.	*Quisiera alquilar una bicicleta.*
I'd like to hire a paddle-boat.	*Quisiera alquilar un barquito de remar.*
Is the tide coming in?	*¿Está subiendo la marea?*
Is it safe to swim here?	*¿Es seguro nadar aquí?*
I'm a beginner at skiing.	*Soy principiate en el esquí.*
I'm intermediate.	*Soy nivel medio.*
I'm very good.	*Soy muy bueno/a.*

Signs

Entrance	*Entrada*
Exit	*Salida*
Open	*Abierto*
Closed	*Cerrado*
Toilets	*Servicios/Aseos*
	(Men – *Hombres*/ Women – *Mujeres*)
Prohibited	*Prohibido*
Danger	*Peligro*
No swimming	*Prohibido nadar*

Additional phrases

Excuse me, madam, you're standing on my foot!	*¡Perdone Señora, pero me está pisando!*
My parents will pay.	*Mis padres van a pagar.*

Good Books

First Thousand Words in Spanish, Heather Amery, Usborne 1995

Spain: A Visual Phrasebook and Dictionary, Collins 2001

Usborne Flashcards – Spanish, Lisa Miles, Usborne 1999

Spain (The Changing Face of…Series), Edward Parker, Hodder 2002

Don Quixote, Miguel de Cervantes, Oxford Classic Tales 2002

Terror on the Amazon, Phil Gates, Dorling Kindersley Eyewitness Readers 2000

Battle of the Spanish Armada, Roger Hart, Hodder 1987

As I Walked Out One Midsummer Morning, Laurie Lee, Penguin 1971

A Rose for Winter, Laurie Lee, Vintage 1999

Homage to Catalonia, George Orwell, Penguin 2000

Asterix in Spain, Goscinny, Hodder 1971

Spain, Julie McCulloch, Heinemann World of Recipes Series 2003

Morbo: The Story of Spanish Football, Phil Ball, When Saturday Comes Books 2003

A Day with Picasso, Susanne Pfleger, Prestel Publishing 1999

The Essential Dalí, Robert Goff, Abrams/Thames and Hudson 1998

The Essential Picasso, Ingrid Schaffner, Abrams/Thames and Hudson 1998

Driving Over Lemons, Chris Stewart, Sort of Books 1999

Mañana, Mañana, Peter Kerr, Summersdale 2001

Wicked
Websites

All sites have English language versions unless indicated otherwise.

www.tourspain.es
This is the Spanish Tourist Board website. It's a great in-depth site with lots of ideas about what to do and see including *fiestas*, what sort of food you'll find in the different regions; maps and photos.

www.spanishfiestas.com
A good, general website about Spain with dates and places for the main *fiestas*.

www.bbc.co.uk/nature
A brief guide to some of Spain's wildlife.

www.bbc.co.uk/weather
Daily weather reports from Spain and a detailed guide to Spain's general climate and regional variations.

www.guggenheim-bilbao.es
The very stylish Guggenheim website.

www.barcelonaturisme.com
Barcelona's What to See and Do Guide.

www.andalucia.com
An excellent regional guide.

www.pamplona.net
Lots of detail about the bull-running festival.

www.patrimonionacional.es
A guide to the Royal Palaces of Spain – where to find them and what their attractions are. Includes virtual tours.

www.telebooks.com
All about Gaudí's amazing buildings with lots of photos.

www.salvador-dali.org
Details and virtual visits of all the Dalí museums.
Quite a whacky site!

www.realmadrid.com
Real Madrid's official site.

www.fcbarcelona.com
Barcelona football team's site.

www.soccer-spain.com
Great website about Spanish football. Up-to-date
details of fixtures and league tables. Has a villains and
heroes section too!

www.lavuelta.com
Great cycling website about the Tour of Spain race. The
posters section is brilliant.

www.top40-charts.com
Up-to-the-minute music charts from around the world.
Includes Spain!

www.madridmusic.com
This site gives dates of forthcoming music festivals
around Spain. Includes all the main festivals. In
Spanish only.

www.cybercaptive.com
A list of Internet cafés in most towns and cities in
Spain.

Quirks and Scribbles